Who Was Blackbeard?

Who Was
Blackbeard?

by James Buckley Jr.
illustrated by Joseph J. M. Qiu

Grosset & Dunlap
An Imprint of Penguin Random House

This is for my friend Paula,
who loves to talk like a pirate with me—JB

I would like to dedicate this book to my wife Esther, my son
Zion, and my parents, who always supported my dream of
working as an artist. To my LORD Jesus Christ who blessed
me with this talent. To the people who I have worked with
and stood by me, love you all—JQ

GROSSET & DUNLAP
Penguin Young Readers Group
An Imprint of Penguin Random House LLC

If you purchased this book without a cover, you should be aware that this book is stolen
property. It was reported as "unsold and destroyed" to the publisher, and neither
the author nor the publisher has received any payment for this "stripped book."

Penguin supports copyright. Copyright fuels creativity, encourages diverse voices,
promotes free speech, and creates a vibrant culture. Thank you for buying an authorized
edition of this book and for complying with copyright laws by not reproducing, scanning,
or distributing any part of it in any form without permission. You are supporting writers
and allowing Penguin to continue to publish books for every reader.

The publisher does not have any control over and does not assume any responsibility for
author or third-party websites or their content.

Text copyright © 2015 by James Buckley Jr. Illustrations copyright © 2015
by Penguin Random House LLC. All rights reserved. Published by Grosset & Dunlap,
an imprint of Penguin Random House LLC, 345 Hudson Street, New York,
New York 10014. Who HQ™ and all related logos are trademarks owned by
Penguin Random House LLC. GROSSET & DUNLAP is a trademark of
Penguin Random House LLC. Printed in the USA.

Library of Congress Cataloging-in-Publication Data is available.

ISBN 978-0-448-48308-5   10 9 8 7 6 5

Contents

Who Was
Blackbeard?

By 1717, Philadelphia was one of the largest
cities in the American colonies, which were
owned by Great Britain. Philadelphia was on the

Delaware River, and its port welcomed ships from Europe almost every day. But in the fall of that year, many of those ships never made it to port. The few that did told tales that shocked and frightened the English colonists in and around Philadelphia. A pirate ship was lurking nearby in the Atlantic Ocean, where the Delaware met the sea.

Captains arriving in New York City and Baltimore told the same stories. A pirate was attacking their ships. He swooped in with his black flag flying. His men stormed merchant ships and stole everything that wasn't nailed down.

The pirate captain himself had a long black beard and wore belts rigged with pistols and swords. He wore lit pieces or rope in his beard so that his face was ringed by smoke. His vessel was equipped with cannons that sent iron balls smashing into the fragile sides of wooden ships. Only a brave few would dare to challenge him and his ferocious crew.

"If speedy care be not taken they will become formidable. . . . Our government can make no defense," wrote Philadelphia merchant James Logan. Captain Charles Johnson later wrote that the pirate had "frightened America more than any comet that has appeared in a long time."

This pirate was causing panic and fear throughout the American colonies. He continued his raids of terror down the Atlantic coast and into the Caribbean Sea. The people that he robbed and captured didn't know it at the time, but they were in the hands of the man who would become the most famous pirate ever: Blackbeard!

Chapter 1
Mysterious Beginnings

The man who became Blackbeard *might* have been born in Bristol, on the southwest coast of England, around the year 1680. Only one record has been found to prove that. The man's real name is a mystery, too. It often appears as Edward Teach. However, it was also written  as Thatch, Tache, Tack, or Thatche.

It does make sense that a man like Teach would have come from a place like Bristol. At that time, Bristol was one of the major ports in England. It is located on the River Avon, which leads to the Atlantic Ocean. Shipbuilders in Bristol were

famous throughout England for the strength
and design of their boats. The busy docks were
crowded with ships and sailors. A boy like Edward
Teach would have found lots to see and do. In
fact, many young boys found jobs on ships as
cabin boys or servants.

Ships left from Bristol for trips to ports all around the world. All those departing ships meant that there was a great need for sailors. Thousands of men from Bristol had become sailors on merchant ships. Others joined the British Royal Navy.

By the 1600s, European countries—including Spain, England, and France—had claimed parts of the Americas and the Caribbean islands as colonies.

British

French

Spanish

AMERICAN COLONIES, 1680

The only way to reach those colonies was by sailing,
so sailors headed west in great numbers. The ships
carried food, clothing, building materials, slaves,
and colonists to the New World. They returned
with sugar, rum, gold, tobacco, and spices.

Edward Teach was said to have fought as a sailor in Queen Anne's War, which lasted from 1702 to 1713. He would have been in his early twenties at the time. England fought this war against Spain and France in Europe and all along the Atlantic coast of its American colonies. Edward did not join the crew of an official Royal

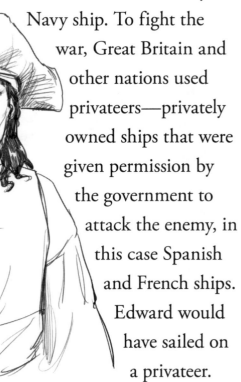

Navy ship. To fight the war, Great Britain and other nations used privateers—privately owned ships that were given permission by the government to attack the enemy, in this case Spanish and French ships. Edward would have sailed on a privateer.

LETTERS OF MARQUE

IF A SHIP'S CAPTAIN WANTED TO BECOME A PRIVATEER, HE ASKED FOR A "LETTER OF MARQUE" (MARK). A LETTER OF MARQUE WAS A GOVERNMENT LICENSE. IT GAVE THE CAPTAIN—AN ORDINARY CIVILIAN—PERMISSION TO ATTACK AND CAPTURE ENEMY SHIPS. MOST COUNTRIES USED PRIVATEERS IN ADDITION TO THEIR OWN NAVIES. THESE PRIVATE SHIPS DIDN'T COST THE GOVERNMENT ANYTHING, AND THEY COULD HELP DISRUPT THE ENEMY BY CAPTURING NECESSARY SUPPLIES. GRANTING A LETTER OF MARQUE WAS AN INEXPENSIVE WAY TO INCREASE A GOVERNMENT'S PRESENCE AT SEA. REQUESTING A LETTER OF MARQUE WAS CONSIDERED A PATRIOTIC CAREER CHOICE.

THE CAPTAIN OF A PRIVATEER COULD KEEP MOST OF WHATEVER HE CAPTURED (KNOWN AS "TAKING PRIZES"), INCLUDING A SHIP AND ALL ITS GOODS. HE AGREED TO PAY THE GOVERNMENT A SMALL PART OF EVERYTHING HE TOOK. UP UNTIL 1708, ENGLAND ASKED FOR 20 PERCENT OF "THE PRIZE."

Captain Johnson wrote that Edward had "uncommon boldness and personal courage" as a sailor.

To serve on such a ship, Edward would have had to master many skills. Sailors needed to be able to navigate, or find their way at sea,

by looking at the stars. They had to memorize the dozens of different ropes and lines they used to raise and lower the sails. They knew how to load, aim, and fire cannons. They shot pistols and muskets, and fought with long and short swords. During his years fighting for England, Edward must have become an expert at all of his duties as a sailor.

When the war ended in 1713, the British letters of marque expired.

Privateers no longer had permission from the king to capture ships and steal their cargo. The problem with privateers was that they often turned into pirates—unlicensed ships filled with sailors cruising the seas for anything they could get their hands on. Governments were then faced with a new problem: trying to capture the same people who had recently been working for them.

By 1716, Edward was working for a pirate named Benjamin Hornigold. He was in charge of seventy men and a boat with six cannons. Edward was in his mid-thirties and not yet well-known, but he had indeed "gone a-pyrating."

Chapter 2
The Pirate Way

Pirates have been a part of life at sea almost since people first started sailing. The ancient Greeks battled pirates as they sailed on the Mediterranean Sea. The ancient Romans fought off pirates who wanted the valuable olive oil carried on Roman ships. The Vikings were pirates of a kind, sailing their warships to raid villages in Europe or capture ships they found at sea.

In the 1500s, English and French pirates called buccaneers sailed the Caribbean Sea. They took their famous name from *buccan*, a Native American word for how the men cooked the meat they ate on their ships. Buccaneers most often attacked Spanish ships and settlements in the Caribbean. English authorities let the buccaneers fight until 1681, when such attacks against Spain were outlawed.

Historians call the early 1700s the "Golden Age of Piracy." Pirates ventured wherever their ships could take them. They did not follow the rules of a navy or a government. Men like Benjamin Hornigold moved about freely, looking for ships to capture.

Many sailors easily "turned pirate" because they could make much more money than if they stayed in the navy. In the navy, a sailor had to do whatever his officers asked of him. If a navy ship captured an enemy ship, the naval officers got most of the cargo and money. Regular sailors received only a small reward. The food on most navy ships was not very good, either. It might have included salted beef that had been stored in barrels for months. The bread was often so hard that it had to be soaked in water to soften it before it could be eaten.

Many sailors died from scurvy because they didn't eat enough fresh vegetables and fruit. It was a hard life.

Pirate ships, on the other hand, were run by all the pirates working together as a committee. They voted one man as captain, but they could vote him out if they didn't like how he ran the ship. All the pirates shared what they stole. And because pirate ships could return to port often, they ate better and fresher food.

SCURVY

SCURVY IS A DISEASE CAUSED BY A LACK OF VITAMIN C. IT WAS VERY COMMON IN THE 1600S AND 1700S, WHEN SAILING SHIPS WERE FAR FROM LAND FOR WEEKS AND MONTHS AT A TIME. SAILORS' TEETH WOULD FALL OUT. THEY WOULD BECOME EXTREMELY TIRED. AND THEIR SKIN WOULD BECOME COVERED IN SPOTS OR SORES. IN THE FIRST HALF OF THE EIGHTEENTH CENTURY, MORE THAN HALF THE DEATHS IN THE BRITISH ROYAL NAVY WERE DUE TO SCURVY, NOT INJURIES RECEIVED IN BATTLE.

FOR MANY YEARS, SHIPS' DOCTORS DID NOT KNOW THE CAUSE OF OR THE CURE FOR SCURVY.

SAILORS WHO ATE FRESH FRUIT OR VEGETABLES SEEMED TO GET SCURVY LESS OFTEN. BUT CARRYING FRESH FOOD WAS DIFFICULT. THERE WERE NO REFRIGERATORS OR ICE TO PRESERVE IT. THE ROYAL NAVY FOUND ONE SOLUTION. THEY BEGAN SERVING LEMON JUICE TO SAILORS ON LONG VOYAGES.

THEY DID NOT UNDERSTAND WHY AT THE TIME, BUT THAT WAS INDEED THE CURE. SAILORS WHO GOT THEIR VITAMIN C FROM LEMON OR LIME JUICE, OR FROM OTHER FRUITS AND VEGETABLES, WERE ABLE TO PREVENT SCURVY.

Pirates and privateers
had homes on land,
but they rarely visited
them. Their ships
became their homes. And they only
went ashore as often as they needed to for supplies
or rest. Some were married, but most did not want
a family to limit their freedom.

Life on any sailing ship in the early 1700s

was still not easy. The men had to sleep on deck
or in hammocks hung in cramped quarters.
They were often wet and cold. There was little
room for storage, so each man could carry only a
few possessions and very few changes of clothes.

Freshwater was scarce, so they rarely bathed. They worked hard hauling ropes and carrying the heavy gear needed to sail the ship.

Though pirates have become famous for looting treasure, most of what they stole was not very exciting. They did take gold, silver, and coins if they found them. But more often their prize was food, new sails for their ships, or the cargo that ships were carrying back and forth to the New World. Their goal was to then sell the cargo—such as cloth, sugar, or rum—for a profit.

Benjamin Hornigold was in charge of several such pirate ships. Like many pirates, Hornigold had been an English privateer during Queen Anne's War. Afterward, he and his pirate crews made their base on the island of New Providence in the Bahamas.

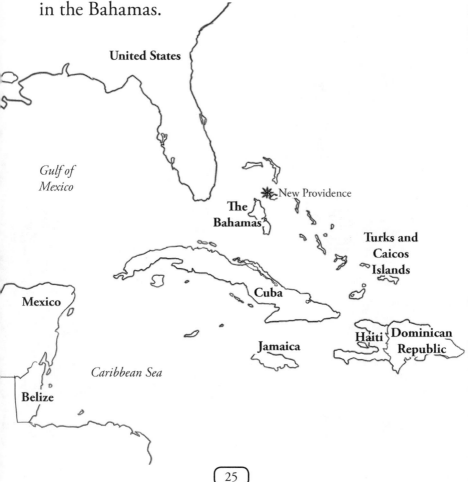

With Hornigold and other pirate captains
acting as governors, the island
became a safe place for
pirates to anchor
between raids.

New Providence had been part of an English colony until the pirates took control of it.

Hornigold was a very successful pirate. It is estimated that in 1715 alone, he and his group of ships captured treasure worth 60,000 British pounds. That's about $12 million in today's money!

Edward Teach became one of Hornigold's top officers. By the end of 1716, he was in command of his own small ship. A year later, Edward would leave Hornigold behind and strike out on his own.

Chapter 3
Captain!

In the fall of 1717, Edward got a chance to move up in the pirate ranks. He and Hornigold met a man named Stede Bonnet. Bonnet was actually an English gentleman, not a rough-and-tumble sailor. He had owned land on the Caribbean island of Barbados, where he grew

STEDE BONNET

sugarcane and had a family. He chose to leave that life behind, however, and become a pirate.

Even though he had never been a sailor, he built a ship, found a crew, and headed toward the coast of the American colonies in search of ships to plunder.

Bonnet's pirating went well at first. He captured four ships in his first weeks as a pirate captain.

When pirates captured a ship, they did one of three things. If they thought they could use the ship and add it to their pirate fleet, they kept it, usually after setting the people on the ship adrift in small boats. Then they moved a pirate crew aboard to run the ship. They sometimes just stole everything from the ship, including the passengers' possessions, and then let it continue its journey.

If they did not want the ship, and they wanted to
send a message to beware, they burned it. Most
pirates let any passengers and sailors escape first,
but a few simply killed them.

Though Bonnet had captured a few ships, he was not a great sailor. So Hornigold took control of Bonnet's ship, the *Revenge*. He then made Edward Teach captain of the *Revenge*. Bonnet remained on board, but only as an assistant to his new captain.

HMS *REVENGE*

The *Revenge* carried twelve large cannons and had 150 sailors on her crew. In the fall, Edward left Hornigold behind and struck out on his own, taking the *Revenge* for himself. He headed north to find ships entering the big ports of the American colonies.

Near Virginia, the *Revenge* stalked and captured
a sloop called the *Betty* and stole all the wine that
the ship was carrying. After putting the passengers
into lifeboats, the crew sank the *Betty*. For the next
several weeks, heading north along the Virginia
and New Jersey coasts, Teach and the *Revenge*
robbed ship after ship. They stole wheat, wine,

sails, ropes for rigging their ships, barrels of meat, and other supplies. Many captains brought reports of a frightening pirate crew back to colonial cities along the coast.

Teach's reputation as a villain was growing. In November 1717, the *Boston News-Letter*

published news from Philadelphia: "Arrived Captain Codd from Liverpool and Dublin. . . . He was taken 12 days since off our cape by a pirate sloop called *Revenge*, of 12 guns, 150 men, commanded by one Teach."

In the fall, Teach turned south toward warmer weather in the Caribbean Sea, in search of new ships to rob.

One of the last ships that Teach captured in 1717 was the *Margaret*. Teach and his men found this merchant ship near the island of Anguilla in early December. They captured the *Margaret*'s crew and held them hostage. They stole the cattle and pigs that the *Margaret* was carrying, along with all the books and sailing instruments owned by the captain, Henry Bostock. Bostock and his crew were eventually released, and they sailed home with their frightening tale.

Bostock told British
officials what had
happened. He had
spent several
hours with
Teach and
gave the first
description of
this now-successful
pirate. "The
Captain . . .
was a tall spare
man with a very black
beard which he wore very long."

That captain—perhaps born Edward Teach and
maybe from Bristol—had become known as the
dreaded pirate Blackbeard.

Chapter 4
Queen Anne's Revenge

As Blackbeard captured more and more ships, he created a small fleet. A fleet is a group of ships that sail together. However, even his growing fleet did not have enough room to hold all the looted cargo.

While sailing near the island of Saint Vincent late in 1717, the *Revenge* and the smaller ships Teach had stolen came upon *La Concorde*. This was a very large French ship packed with slaves. The slaves had been captured in what is now the country of Benin in Africa. The ship was carrying them to markets in French colonies such as Haiti and Martinique, where they would be sold to plantation owners. To make room for more slaves on board, many of its cannons had been left behind.

La Concorde had been at sea for more than two months. More than fifty of the five hundred slaves had already died on the journey. The crew members of the ship were very sick. Many had scurvy. Only a few were healthy enough to sail the ship . . . or fight off a pirate attack.

On November 28, 1717, the lookouts high atop the masts of the *Revenge* spotted the sails of the slave ship. Blackbeard ordered his helmsman, the sailor steering the ship, to head toward the sails in the distance. The small *Revenge* was a fast-moving ship, so there was no escape for *La Concorde*.

THE SLAVE TRADE

WHEN EUROPEAN COUNTRIES FORMED COLONIES IN THE WARMER AREAS OF THE NEW WORLD, THE COLONISTS ESTABLISHED PLANTATIONS. THESE WERE LARGE FARMS THAT RAISED CROPS SUCH AS RICE, SUGARCANE, TOBACCO, AND COTTON. THEY NEEDED A LOT OF PEOPLE TO WORK ON THOSE GIANT FARMS. THEY WANTED TO KEEP PRODUCTION LEVELS HIGH, AND COSTS LOW. IN ORDER TO MAKE THE MOST PROFIT FROM THEIR LAND AND CROPS, THEY DID NOT WANT TO PAY PEOPLE TO WORK ON THE PLANTATIONS.

BEGINNING IN THE 1500S, NATIONS SUCH AS GREAT BRITAIN, THE NETHERLANDS, FRANCE, PORTUGAL, AND SPAIN CAPTURED PEOPLE ALONG THE WEST COAST OF AFRICA. SLAVE TRADERS LOADED THEM ONTO SHIPS AND TOOK THEM TO THE NEW WORLD COLONIES. THE VOYAGE WAS AWFUL FOR THE AFRICANS. THEY HAD VERY LITTLE ROOM ON THE BOATS, OFTEN NOT EVEN ENOUGH TO STAND. THEY WERE GIVEN ALMOST NO FOOD OR WATER,

AND THEY WERE OFTEN VERY SICK. THOUSANDS
DIED EVERY YEAR AT SEA, LONG BEFORE THE
SHIPS HAD REACHED THEIR FINAL DESTINATIONS.

ONCE THE CAPTIVES ARRIVED IN THE COLONIES,
THEY WERE SOLD AS
SLAVES TO
WORK IN
THE FIELDS.
SLAVES WERE
TREATED AS
PROPERTY, AND
BOUGHT AND SOLD
LIKE CATTLE. THEY
HAD NO RIGHTS AND WERE OFTEN SEPARATED FROM
THEIR FAMILIES.

VERY SLOWLY, OTHER PEOPLE BEGAN TO REALIZE
HOW HORRIBLE AND UNFAIR SLAVERY WAS. FRANCE
ENDED SLAVERY IN ITS COLONIES IN 1794. GREAT
BRITAIN ABOLISHED ITS SLAVE TRADE IN 1807.
SLAVERY DID NOT END EVERYWHERE IN THE UNITED
STATES UNTIL THE CIVIL WAR WAS OVER, IN 1865.

IT IS UNCERTAIN HOW MANY PEOPLE WERE
CAPTURED IN AFRICA FROM THE 1500S TO THE
1800S. SOME ESTIMATES ARE AS HIGH AS TWELVE
MILLION.

Soon the *Revenge* reached the French ship, which
was moving slowly through the water. Blackbeard
ordered cannons to be loaded and pushed into
place at their windows on the side of the ship.

As the *Revenge* moved even closer to *La Concorde*, he ordered the cannons to fire. All the cannons on one side of the *Revenge* fired at once, a volley known as a broadside. A dozen iron cannonballs smashed into *La Concorde*!

Huge wooden planks and splinters broke off and flew through the air, killing some of the French sailors. Other balls tore through the ropes that held up sails, which crashed down to the deck. Without sails to catch the wind, *La Concorde* was unable to move. Blackbeard had captured a major prize.

Blackbeard did not free the Africans. Although he allowed a few to join his pirate crew, he gave the rest back to the French captain, who carried them to the island of Martinique to be sold.

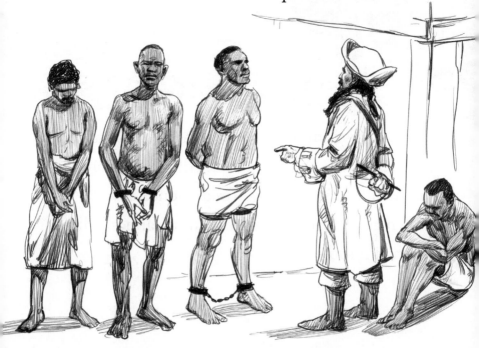

The pirate crew swarmed over their new ship. Blackbeard took command and renamed it the *Queen Anne's Revenge*. As the largest ship in his pirate fleet, the *Queen Anne's Revenge* became Blackbeard's flagship, or lead ship.

He and his men rebuilt parts of the ship to make it better for pirating. They removed many of the smaller cabins to make room for more cannons. They changed the sails and rigging to make the ship faster.

Then Blackbeard split up his crew to sail all the ships now under his command. With the addition of his new prize, Captain Blackbeard now controlled as many as three hundred men and more than fifty cannons.

Chapter 5
The Blockade of Charleston

Blackbeard now controlled one of the largest pirate ships afloat. He gave himself a new title, commodore, because he felt he now deserved a rank above a captain. In the navy, a commodore is a person in command of an entire fleet.

With his new ships, Blackbeard sailed west to Central America.

Off the coast of what is now Belize, he captured the small British ship *Adventure*, and added its twelve guns to his total. Blackbeard sailed along the Central American coast, finding and capturing several other small vessels.

At one point, a large British ship called the *Protestant Caesar* tried to outsail the *Queen Anne's Revenge*. Blackbeard did not want to give up even one opportunity to seize supplies and treasure, so he chased down the ship. When the frightened crew saw Blackbeard's flag flying above the ship bearing 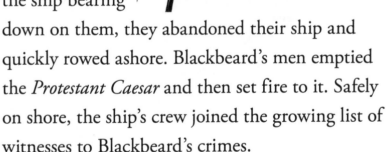 down on them, they abandoned their ship and quickly rowed ashore. Blackbeard's men emptied the *Protestant Caesar* and then set fire to it. Safely on shore, the ship's crew joined the growing list of witnesses to Blackbeard's crimes.

PIRATE FLAGS

AT SEA, FLAGS WERE THE BEST WAY TO IDENTIFY A SHIP. NAVY SHIPS FLEW THEIR COUNTRY'S FLAG. PIRATE SHIPS WAITED UNTIL THEY NEARED THEIR PREY AND THEN RAISED A BLACK FLAG—THE EUROPEAN AND AMERICAN SIGN FOR PIRATES.

PIRATES DECORATED THEIR BLACK FLAGS IN DIFFERENT WAYS. THE MOST POPULAR SYMBOL WAS A SKULL AND CROSSBONES, KNOWN AS THE JOLLY ROGER.

BLACKBEARD'S OWN BLACK FLAG FEATURED A SMILING SKELETON HOLDING A SPEAR THAT POINTED AT A BLOODRED HEART.

Creating a fierce reputation had been a big part of Blackbeard's plan. By this time, he rarely engaged in battles at sea. Once sailors realized it was Blackbeard who was attacking, they almost always surrendered in fear. Blackbeard himself was growing as bold as his reputation. With each conquest, he seemed to take bigger and bigger risks.

In May 1718, Blackbeard did something no
pirate had tried before: He blockaded an entire
port. He sailed his ships into the harbor entrance
of Charleston (then called Charles Town), South
Carolina. Charles Town was a large and busy port.

The colony of South Carolina shipped rice, indigo (a plant used to make blue dye), tobacco, and other crops to England. In just a few days, Blackbeard captured as many as ten ships trying to enter or leave the harbor. He locked his prisoners in the hold—the cargo deck—of his ship after stealing everything they carried. He emptied the captured ships of all their goods. Once Blackbeard's blockade was in place, no ships dared to leave port. The ship owners worried that the rice would rot on board the ships as they sat in the harbor.

HARBOR BLOCKADE

FOR CENTURIES, BLOCKADING A CITY WAS A BIG PART OF WARFARE. ON THE SEA, SHIPS LINED UP TO BLOCK A HARBOR ENTRANCE. NO FOOD OR SUPPLIES COULD PASS THE BLOCKADE, NOR COULD TROOPS ARRIVE TO HELP. PORT CITIES MIGHT STILL RECEIVE HELP FROM LAND, BUT OFTEN THAT HELP WAS MANY DAYS OR WEEKS AWAY, AS TRAVEL BY LAND WAS VERY SLOW.

SOMETIMES BLOCKADES LASTED FOR MONTHS, UNTIL A TOWN RAN OUT OF FOOD OR WATER AND HAD TO SURRENDER JUST TO SURVIVE.

For more than a week, Blackbeard and his fleet captured ship after ship coming into the port. Finally, he sent a message to the city's leaders that he needed medicine for his crew. He threatened to murder his prisoners and send their heads back to the city if they did not meet his demands.

GOVERNOR
ROBERT JOHNSON

In a report, South Carolina governor Robert Johnson wrote that the pirates "appeared in sight of the town, took our pilot boat and afterwards 8 or 9 sail [ships] with several of the best inhabitants of this place on board and then sent me word if I did not immediately send them a chest of medicines they would put every prisoner to death. . . . This company is commanded by one Teach alias Blackbeard [who] has a ship of 40 odd guns under him and . . . are in all above 400 men."

Not surprisingly, the city's leaders agreed immediately.

Blackbeard sent a prisoner and two pirates into Charles Town to collect the medicine. Several days went by, and the men did not return. He sent another group of crewmen to look for them. The search party discovered that the first two pirates had gone drinking instead of bringing the medicine back to the ship.

Once all the pirates were safely aboard, Blackbeard let the hostages return to Charles Town. He did keep all their money and jewelry and most of their fine clothes. After receiving the medicine, Blackbeard kept his word and left the port of Charles Town.

The news of the blockade of Charles Town traveled up and down the coast. Blackbeard had become colonial America's public enemy number one. The news that he had taken control of one of its busiest ports had reached England. The British government, which owned and controlled the colonies, knew that something had to be done. They began to make plans to bring Blackbeard to justice.

Chapter 6
A Short Time Ashore

After leaving Charles Town, Blackbeard sailed north. He needed a place to rest his crew and repair their ships. His fleet headed to the barrier islands of North Carolina. The tiny bays and narrow waterways between islands were perfect places to hide from navy ships.

As the huge *Queen Anne's Revenge* tried to sail nearer to the coast, it ran aground on a sandbar—the bottom of the ship smashed into the bottom of the shallow sea.

The mighty ship was badly damaged. It could not be towed out of the sand and would soon sink.

WHO OWNED THE NEW WORLD?

WHEN QUEEN ANNE'S WAR ENDED IN 1713, A HANDFUL OF EUROPEAN COUNTRIES CONTROLLED DIFFERENT PARTS OF THE NEW WORLD.

ON THE NORTH AMERICAN MAINLAND, ALL BUT ONE OF THE ORIGINAL THIRTEEN AMERICAN COLONIES HAD BEEN ESTABLISHED FOR ENGLAND. (GEORGIA DID NOT JOIN UNTIL 1732.) EACH OF THE COLONIES HAD ITS OWN GOVERNOR, WHO ENFORCED THE KING'S LAWS. ENGLAND ALSO OWNED SOME OF THE CARIBBEAN ISLANDS, INCLUDING JAMAICA, BERMUDA, AND THE BAHAMAS.

SPAIN CONTROLLED WHAT IS NOW FLORIDA UNTIL 1821. THEY ESTABLISHED MEXICO AND MOST OF CENTRAL AMERICA AS SPANISH COLONIES. SPAIN OWNED THE ISLANDS OF CUBA AND PUERTO RICO.

FRANCE, MEANWHILE, LOST SOME OF ITS
COLONIES TO ENGLAND AFTER THE WAR. IT KEPT
PART OF THE NORTH AMERICAN MAINLAND, FROM
CANADA DOWN TO THE GULF OF MEXICO, AS WELL
AS THE CARIBBEAN ISLANDS OF GUADELOUPE AND
MARTINIQUE, AS WELL AS THE NATION THAT LATER
BECAME KNOWN AS HAITI.

Blackbeard ordered the ship emptied of as
much stolen cargo, supplies, and sailing gear as
possible. It was all loaded onto a smaller ship
called the *Adventure*. While the pirate crew was
transferring their treasure, they learned of some
very interesting news from England.

Charles Eden, the governor of the colony of
North Carolina, was offering a royal pardon for
pirates. Given by King George I of England,
the pardon forgave all British pirates. It was a
way to get the pirates to stop stealing without
having to attack or capture them. Blackbeard sent
Stede Bonnet, who had remained on board the
Revenge all this time, to request a pardon from the
governor of the North Carolina colony.

But while Bonnet was on his way back from seeing the governor, Blackbeard sailed away in the *Adventure*, along with all the treasure and cargo Bonnet and his men owned. Blackbeard marooned, or left behind, most of the crew on a small island. Blackbeard the pirate was now stealing from other pirates!

Blackbeard sailed with his smaller force to the town of Bath, North Carolina. He wanted to meet Governor Eden personally. Blackbeard convinced the governor to not only pardon him and his men but also to

GOVERNOR EDEN

help them. Blackbeard said that he and his men would protect the small town from other pirates.

In return, Eden would give them a place to live in the colony.

For several months, the men of the sea became men of the land. They built small houses in Bath and met the townspeople. Bath itself was not very big, perhaps no more than two dozen homes in all,

so the arrival of the pirates increased the population quite a bit. The pirates were not perfect citizens, and rumors of wild parties and troublemaking followed them. Governor Eden ignored the trouble, probably because the pirates were paying him with some of the gold or supplies they had stolen.

A local legend says that Blackbeard himself built a house on Plum Point, overlooking the town harbor. But he spent a lot of time making trips to his ship, which was anchored nearby.

That was because, even though he had been officially forgiven for his crimes, Blackbeard still continued raiding passing ships! Two of the ships that Blackbeard captured while living in Bath were from France. One was carrying sugar back to Europe.

On August 23, 1718, Blackbeard sailed toward the two large merchant ships, his cannons pointing straight ahead. Suddenly, as if scared, he steered his craft away. While the Frenchmen watched this odd display, what they did not see was another of Blackbeard's boats coming up from the other side. Musket balls suddenly whizzed over the heads of the French crew. Then Blackbeard returned to trap the two ships between his own craft. It was another example of his brilliant sailing and ruthless pirating skills. Pardoned or not, Blackbeard couldn't seem to give up the life of a fortune hunter.

Chapter 7
The Hunt Is On

Though Governor Eden was not hunting Blackbeard, and was in fact sharing some of his profits, other governors in the colonies still wanted the pirate's head. William Keith, the governor of Pennsylvania, ordered him arrested . . . if someone could find him. Alexander Spotswood, the governor of Virginia, tried but couldn't locate him.

GOVERNOR SPOTSWOOD

Spotswood was outraged by the capture of the French ships and by Governor Eden's behavior in helping the pirates. "I thought it necessary to put a stop to further progress of the robberies," he wrote.

Only one of Blackbeard's men, William Howard, was captured and arrested by Spotswood's officers. Howard gave up information about where Blackbeard might be. Governor Spotswood ordered two Royal Navy ships to sail to North Carolina with orders to find and capture or kill Blackbeard.

Blackbeard, meanwhile, remained in North
Carolina. By this time, he had moved out of Bath
and spent most of his time in a camp on Ocracoke
Island, one of the barrier islands of North Carolina.

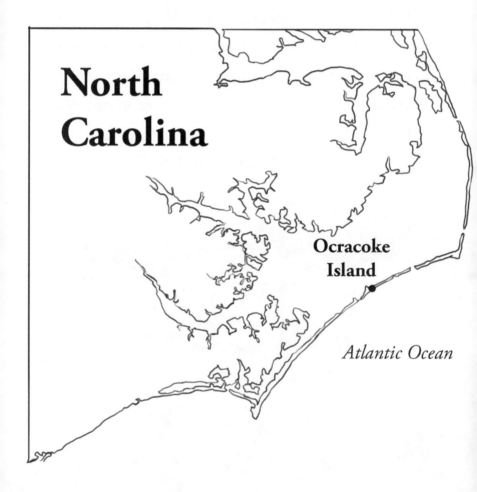

North
Carolina

Ocracoke
Island

Atlantic Ocean

Formed mostly of sand, the islands shrink and
grow over time as they are battered by waves and
tides. Few trees or grasses grow on the dunes,
and only seabirds lived there at the time. The
wind howls often and the nights can be cold.

Blackbeard's crew would have made camp using ships' sails for tents and cooking over campfires. He was probably aware that British ships were searching for him, but he believed that he had picked a good hiding spot. The narrow inlets around the island would make it hard for large ships to reach him.

At the same time, more and more Royal Navy ships were indeed patrolling the waters off the American mainland and near the British colonies of the Caribbean. The net was closing around the pirates.

Chapter 8
The Death of Blackbeard

Ships on the North Carolina coast reported seeing Blackbeard and his crew camped on Ocracoke Island. It would be tricky to reach the camp. The pirates had anchored their small ship, the *Adventure,* down a very narrow channel of water. The large Royal Navy ships could not sail near the island without hitting bottom.

Captain Ellis Brand of HMS *Pearl* put Lieutenant Robert Maynard in charge of the attack. (HMS stands for His Majesty's Ship. "His Majesty," in this case, refers to England's King George I.) Maynard hired two smaller ships, the *Ranger* and the *Jane.* They

ROBERT MAYNARD

were lighter and would be able to navigate in the shallow water.

Brand told Maynard and his crew that there was a hundred-pound reward for Blackbeard (about $20,000 today) as well as smaller amounts to be paid for other captured pirates. Earning that reward would be very dangerous, however.

Maynard hired two local men as pilots. They knew the channels and sandbars very well. The pilots would help the sailors aboard the *Ranger* and the *Jane* make it to the small bay near Blackbeard's camp on Ocracoke.

On the cloudy morning of November 22, 1718, the two ships sailed toward Blackbeard's anchored ship. Blackbeard and his men had been drinking until early that morning. He was probably still asleep. But when a lookout spotted the navy ships, Blackbeard and his men rallied to action.

The *Ranger* and the *Jane* fast approached the *Adventure*. When they were only a few hundred yards from the pirates, Maynard's ships unfurled their flags—Union Jacks, the symbol of Great Britain. The pirates knew for sure that they were being hunted by the British Royal Navy.

Maynard called over the water for the pirates to surrender. He said later that Blackbeard yelled back and insulted his men. The dreaded pirate called Maynard and his men "cowardly puppies" and said he would "neither give nor take quarter."

Quarter can mean one-fourth of something or it can mean mercy. Blackbeard used it to mean he would neither give any mercy to nor expect any mercy from his attackers.

Blackbeard backed up his words by firing a broadside at the two navy ships. The cannons were loaded with iron balls, nails, and scrap iron.

The red-hot pieces of metal tore into the navy ships. With one blast, more than twenty men out of only fifty-seven crew members were killed or wounded on the *Jane* and the *Ranger*.

Maynard was on board the *Jane*. He saw that many of his men were injured or dead. His small ships had no cannons to fire back. They had left them behind so the ships would be light enough to reach Blackbeard. To save his men from another broadside, he sent many of them down into the hold, below the deck of the ship.

Blackbeard steered his ship toward the *Jane*. He thought most of Maynard's men were dead, and that he could storm and capture the ship. As they got nearer, Blackbeard's men threw grenadoes that exploded on the deck of the *Jane*. (A grenado was a small explosive that could be thrown at a target, similar to a hand grenade.)

When the sides of the two ships banged together, the pirates threw metal hooks over the *Jane*'s rails. The ropes attached to the hooks tied the two ships together. Blackbeard led the way across onto the *Jane*. He was wearing his pistols and waving a huge sword.

Maynard and a handful of men faced the large
group of pirates.

Suddenly, the rest of the *Jane*'s crew burst from
the hold. Blackbeard's crew was outnumbered.
A desperate fight followed. Pirates and sailors
used swords, pistols, axes, and even wooden poles
to fight each other. The deck grew slippery with
seawater and blood. In the middle of the battle,
Lieutenant Maynard and Blackbeard faced off.

Maynard shot Blackbeard with a pistol, but the pirate stayed on his feet. The two men clashed swords. Even though he had been wounded, Blackbeard was so strong that he broke Maynard's sword. Maynard grabbed another pistol and shot Blackbeard again. By then, other sailors were running to help Maynard. A navy sailor slashed at Blackbeard's face, leaving a large wound. But the pirate kept fighting.

For several moments, Blackbeard battled against the sailors before he finally fell to the deck. After being shot five times and stabbed with swords twenty times, Blackbeard was dead. He was probably no more than forty years old.

A few minutes later, the other pirates surrendered.

The navy sailors locked the captured and shackled pirates in the holds of the *Ranger* and the *Jane*. They made sure all the dead pirates' bodies were brought aboard, too. They would need them to collect their money. The reward would be paid for any pirate, alive or dead.

Maynard had Blackbeard's head cut off. The legendary pirate's body was thrown into the ocean. A local legend says that it swam around the ship three times before sinking forever into the Atlantic. Blackbeard's head was hung from the front of the *Jane*.

The British government did not treat pirates kindly. The punishment was death. The survivors from Blackbeard's crew were brought to Virginia and put on trial. All but two were convicted and hanged.

Like many executed pirates, their bodies were then hung near the entrance to the harbor in Virginia. Colonial leaders displayed the rotting corpses, often pecked apart by birds, as a warning to any other would-be pirates.

When Maynard returned to what is now Hampton, Virginia, in triumph, Blackbeard's head was stuck on a tall pole for everyone to see. Today, the spot where his head was on view is known as Blackbeard's Point.

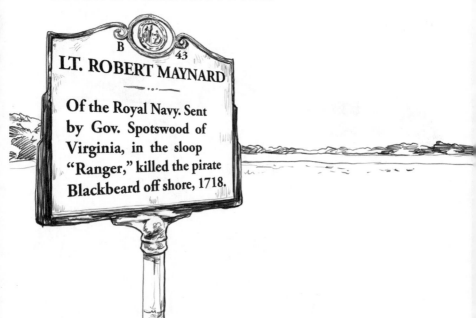

B 43
LT. ROBERT MAYNARD

Of the Royal Navy. Sent by Gov. Spotswood of Virginia, in the sloop "Ranger," killed the pirate Blackbeard off shore, 1718.

Chapter 9
Blackbeard's Legacy

In 1724, a book was published that helped
make Blackbeard and many
other pirates famous. Written in
England by a man named Charles
Johnson (which historians think
was probably not his real name),
*A General History of the Robberies
and Murders of the Most Notorious
Pyrates* told tales of pirates on the
high seas, raids on ships, and the treasures they
captured. Johnson's book is one of the only places
that Edward Teach is called Blackbeard. But the
image Johnson described made Blackbeard clear in
the reader's mind: the belt of pistols, the enormous
smoking beard, and Blackbeard's fiery eyes.

Because no paintings or drawings of Blackbeard were made while he was alive, many of the images we're now familiar with were based on Johnson's descriptions.

Those pictures helped spread the Blackbeard legend. Creating that legend was a big part of Blackbeard's life. He worked hard to create a fearsome look. His long, wild beard was said to cover most of his face. He wore not one or two but many swords and pistols when he went into battle. He burned ships, stole whatever he could take, and threatened people with death. It was rumored that he even shot at his fellow pirates to keep them in line. But in reality, it is not known that Blackbeard ever killed any of the prisoners he took.

He released his hostages. And he actually let some ships go on their way if they did not have much for him to steal. For a short time, at least, he settled into a life on land in a house in Bath. One account even says that he was married there.

Still, the legend of Blackbeard lives on. Unfortunately, piracy has never really gone away. In recent years, pirates from East Africa have attacked and captured ships in the Indian Ocean, including large oil tankers and luxury yachts. They steal money they find on board or steal the contents of the tankers, including the valuable oil. Today's pirates use fast motorboats to catch and overtake the slow-moving tankers.

PIRATE MYTHS

SINCE THE GOLDEN AGE OF PIRACY, MANY MYTHS AND LEGENDS ABOUT PIRATES HAVE SPRUNG UP. HISTORIANS HAVE BEEN ABLE TO SHOW THAT SOME OF THE MOST FAMOUS PIRATE TALES IN THE WORLD ARE NOT TRUE AT ALL.

WILLIAM KIDD

- ONLY ONE PIRATE, CAPTAIN WILLIAM KIDD, WAS ALLEGED TO HAVE BURIED TREASURE. IN FACT, MOST PIRATES NEVER MADE SO MUCH MONEY THAT THEY COULD AFFORD TO LEAVE SOME BEHIND. THEY NEEDED IT TO BUY FOOD, AMMUNITION, AND RUM.

- PIRATES DID NOT SAY "ARRR!" THAT NOW-FAMOUS WORD WAS FIRST USED IN A 1950 MOVIE VERSION OF ROBERT LOUIS STEVENSON'S FAMOUS PIRATE BOOK, *TREASURE ISLAND*. THE ACTOR ROBERT NEWTON PLAYED PIRATE CAPTAIN LONG JOHN SILVER. NEWTON BASED HIS ACCENT ON MEN FROM THE SOUTHWEST COAST OF ENGLAND, WHERE IT'S BELIEVED MANY PIRATES SAILED FROM.

- THERE IS ALMOST NO HISTORICAL RECORD OF PIRATES MAKING PRISONERS "WALK THE PLANK." THOUGH SOME PIRATES DID KILL THEIR HOSTAGES, MOST LET THEM GO.

Blackbeard and other pirates continue to have a huge impact on modern culture. Pirates have always been popular in movies. As early as the 1920s and 1930s, films like *The Sea Hawk* and *Captain Blood* told tales of pirates at sea. Burt Lancaster starred in the exciting film *The Crimson Pirate* in 1952. And a comedy called *Blackbeard's Ghost* came out in 1968. More recently, the success of the Pirates of the Caribbean movie series made pirate lore and legend popular once again.

People enjoy the legends surrounding pirates such as Blackbeard. Historians, however, look for the facts.

PIRATES OF THE CARIBBEAN

ONE OF THE MOST POPULAR RIDES AT DISNEYLAND OPENED IN 1967. PIRATES OF THE CARIBBEAN TAKES VISITORS INTO A MAKE-BELIEVE WORLD BASED ON THE GOLDEN AGE OF PIRACY. CANNONS BLAST, PIRATES COUNT THEIR TREASURE, AND A CITY IS ATTACKED.

IN 2003, WALT DISNEY STUDIOS MADE A MOVIE BASED ON THE RIDE AND ON MANY PIRATE LEGENDS. ACTOR JOHNNY DEPP PLAYS THE FICTIONAL CAPTAIN JACK SPARROW. CHARACTERS BASED ON PIRATES FROM HISTORY MAKE APPEARANCES IN THE FILMS, SUCH AS THE CHINESE PIRATE CHARACTER OF SAO FENG. BLACKBEARD WAS PLAYED BY THE ACTOR IAN MCSHANE IN *ON STRANGER TIDES,* THE FOURTH MOVIE IN THE SERIES.

A TOTAL OF FOUR FILMS IN THE SERIES HAVE BEEN RELEASED, AND A FIFTH IS PLANNED FOR 2017.

In 1996, divers working underwater off the coast of North Carolina discovered the wreck of a large sailing ship. Artifacts they found made them believe they had located the last resting place of Blackbeard's famous ship, the *Queen*

Anne's Revenge. They found cannonballs, coins, bells, medical gear, and other artifacts. One of the cannons was fully loaded, ready for firing. After fifteen years of careful study, officials confirmed that the wreck was indeed Blackbeard's ship.

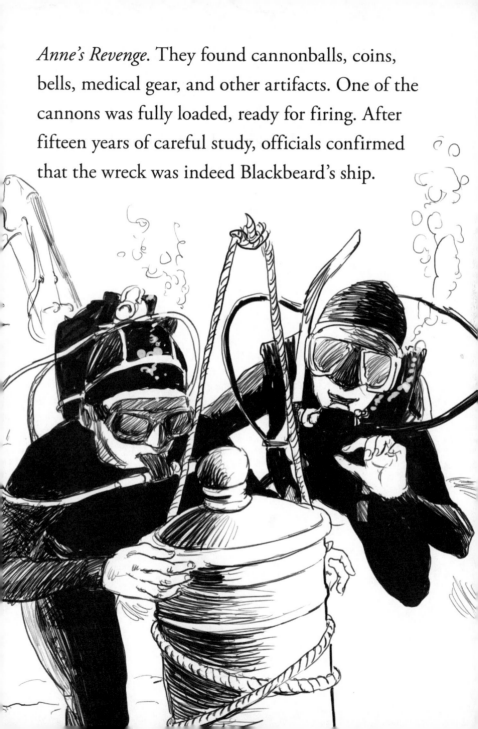

But while the pirate's ship has been found, the mystery around this bearded villain remains. Though it is not known for certain how he began, it *is* known how Blackbeard ended—as the most famous pirate in history.

TIMELINE OF
BLACKBEARD'S LIFE

c. 1680 ——— Edward Teach is born, possibly in Bristol, England

1713 ——— Finishes service on a privateer ship in Queen Anne's War

1716 ——— Becomes an assistant under pirate Benjamin Hornigold

1717 ——— Becomes captain of the *Revenge*, his first solo command
Attacks ships off eastern American colonies near Philadelphia
Captures *La Concorde* near Caribbean island of Saint Vincent and renames it the *Queen Anne's Revenge*

1718 ——— Names himself commodore
Attacks ships in the Caribbean and also near Central America
In May, returns to the Atlantic and blockades the harbor of Charles Town, South Carolina, for more than a week
In November, killed in battle against the Royal Navy near Ocracoke Island, North Carolina

TIMELINE OF THE WORLD

Death of Kateri Tekakwitha, the first Native — 1680
American Catholic saint

Pennsylvania colony is founded by William Penn — 1681

Salem witch trials held in Massachusetts Bay Colony — 1692

Thomas Savery patents the first practical steam engine — 1698

Queen Anne's War begins among England, Spain, — 1702
and France

Benjamin Franklin is born in Boston, Massachusetts — 1706

The United Kingdom is formed when the Act of Union — 1707
unites England, Scotland, and Wales

During the Great Frost, Europe suffers through — 1709
its coldest winter in five centuries

Queen Anne's War ends with the treaties of Utrecht — 1713

City of New Orleans is founded by French settlers — 1718

Robinson Crusoe, by Daniel Defoe, is published — 1719

BIBLIOGRAPHY

Bourne, Joel K., Jr. "Scourge of the Atlantic: Blackbeard the Pirate." **National Geographic: Exploring History**, Winter 2013, 16.

Cabell, Craig, and Graham Thomas. **Blackbeard: The Hunt for the World's Notorious Pirate**. South Yorkshire, England: Pen & Sword Maritime, 2012.

* Croce, Pat. **Blackbeard**. Philadelphia: Running Press Classics, 2011.

Konstam, Angus. **Blackbeard: America's Most Notorious Pirate**. Hoboken, NJ: Wiley, 2006.

* Platt, Richard. **Eyewitness Books: Pirate**. New York: DK Publishing, 2007.

Woodard, Colin. "The Last Days of Blackbeard." **Smithsonian**, February 2014, 32.

* Books for young readers